BARDO TEACHINGS

The Way of Death and Rebirth

Revised Edition
by
Venerable Lama Lodö

Foreword by
The Very Venerable Kalu Rinpoche

SNOW LION PUBLICATIONS
Ithaca, New York USA

Snow Lion Publications
P.O. Box 6483
Ithaca, New York 14851
USA

First published by KDK Publications, San Francisco, 1982.
First Snow Lion Publications edition, 1987.

Printed in USA

Library of Congress Catalog Number

ISBN 0-937938-60-2

Library of Congress Cataloging-in-Publication Data

Lodru Lama.
    Bardo Teachings.

    Bibliography: p.
   · 1. Intermediate state—Buddhism.   2. Death—
Religious aspects—Buddhism.   3. Buddhism—China—Tibet.
I. Title.
BQ4490.L67   1987   294.3'423   87-20663
ISBN 0-937938-60-2

Contents

The Very Venerable Kalu Rinpoche
wearing the ceremonial Gampopa Hat.
Photograph taken at Kagyu Ling Retreat Center, Plaige, France.

**This book is dedicated to the
Very Venerable Kalu Rinpoche
for the Benefit of All Sentient Beings.**

ༀགམརདབྱུངགུནཁྱབ

Vénérable KHEMPO KALOU RIMPOTCHÉ

Foreword

I should like to acquaint all those people whose support for the Buddhadharma derives from noble aspirations and positive karmic connections, with this work written by my disciple Lama Lodö. In writing these descriptions of three aspects of bardo, he has wished to benefit others, and these words of Lama Lodö can be considered authentic and in accord with the Bardo Thodol cycle and the writings of teachers such as Karma Chagme Rinpoche. In the hope that everyone will benefit greatly from these teachings, I would ask all concerned to approach them with this in mind. I speak as one who regards all traditions of the Buddha's teachings with the utmost respect.

Samdrub Thargay Ling Monastery
P.O. Sonada 734219
Darjeeling, W. Bengal
India

Acknowledgments

As the editors, it has been our privilege to work with Lama Lodö. He has been continually generous and patient, sharing his time and knowledge with us. As his students, we feel very fortunate to be able to devote our time and experience to his book which advances the teaching of the Dharma in the West.

Many of Lama Lodö's students contributed to the publication of this edition. Drölma Chötso (Sheila Sullivan) drew the Buddhas appearing in Chapter Two. Michael Conklin assisted with the English translation of the Glossary. Karma Chösky Gyamtso (Joseph Duane, Esq.) and Karma Pema Khandro (Dr. Corina Meyer) provided the material for Lama Lodo's biography. Karma Sonam Chotso (Kira Henriksen) transcribed the revised material.

We thank all these individuals for their dedication and work, and Snow Lion Publications for bringing out this latest edition.

We wish to dedicate any merit received towards the enlightenment of all sentient beings.

The Editors,
Karma Pema Zangmo (Nancy Clark)
Karma Yeshe Chö Dön (Caroline Parke)

Kagyu Suka Choling
Eugene, Oregon

Preface

During the winter of 1978, at the direction of Very Venerable Kalu Rinpoche, Venerable Lama Lodö (pronounced "Lodru"), resident Lama at Kagyu Droden Kunchab in San Francisco, presented a series of teachings on the *Bardo Thodol*. The teachings were in Tibetan and were translated by Dawa Norbu and Janet Gyatso. Subsequently, many requests for tapes of the talks were received, but since some parts of the recordings were not clear, Lama Lodö decided instead to produce a small book for those who wished to learn the basic Bardo teachings. The tapes were intitially transcribed by Okanta Leonard. This manuscript was then checked and clarified by Lama Lodö, assisted by Yeshe Dargye and Tsering Zangmo (Ken and Donna McVicar).

Kagyu Droden Kunchab
San Francisco
1979

Introductory Note
by
Lama Lodö

In the teachings that follow, we are going to deal with the Chikai Bardo and the Sipai Bardo. I received the oral transmission on these from Very Venerable Kalu Rinpoche and also studied the description of the Sipai Bardo in the *Dharma of Solitude* by Chagme Rinpoche. The Chonyi Bardo will not be presented in detail; it is dealt with very clearly in the work of Trungpa Rinpoche and Francesca Fremantle, which should be consulted by those who are interested. It is also included in the translation by Kazi Dawa-Samdup edited by Evans-Wentz. The teachings on the Chikai Bardo, however, have not previously been published in translation. Now that these precious scriptures are being made available, you will all realize the usefulness of Vajrayana teachings in attaining liberation.

The reason we call the Vajrayana the "secret path" is because it contains very special methods, making it possible to attain instantaneous enlightenment. These methods are so easy that many people will not believe them, and so deep that most people cannot understand them. If the methods are revealed to one whose mind is not prepared by Dharma practice, then it will create danger for both the teacher and the student. It will be dangerous for the teacher because he gave the teaching without closely examining his disciple, and for the student because he will not believe the methods and will have wrong views of the path.

If the Buddhas appear suddenly to us at the time of death, then our enlightenment could occur spontaneously and instantaneously. The basic point of the whole teaching is: *recognizing what is occurring is the key to gaining enlightenment.* If during this lifetime we accumulate a great deal of negative karma and have little faith in the fact of enlightenment, then when we die, the weight of our heavy karma will keep us from recognizing the deities. This means there is no chance to gain liberation. It is a grave mistake to believe that we can achieve recognition of the deities in the Bardo without great effort in this lifetime. It is of the utmost importance right now to accumulate merit by practicing compassion and fostering devotion to the Buddha. In addition, it is essential to meditate well and to visualize the deities as clearly as possible. Then we will be able to attain enlightenment in the Bardo through positive habitual tendencies acquired during this lifetime.

Now is the time for you to read, learn, and practice to reach enlightenment for the benefit of all beings. Those of you who have had the initiation into the Hundred Deities of the Bardo, the *lung* and the instruction, should practice the meditation of *Dorje Sempa* in order to keep your commitments. The Hundred Syllable Mantra is the essence of the Hundred Deities of the Bardo.

Through these teachings may all beings be liberated from the ocean of Samsara.

EDITOR'S NOTE: Foreign words are italicized in first use, as are names of the Buddhas and Bodhisattvas, and various technical terms. Exceptions to this rule are "Buddha," "Dharma," "Lama," "Karma," "Samsara," "Tantra," "Mantra," and "Vajrayana," as they are well on their way to being integrated into the English language. Tibetan and Sanskrit words are indicated by the abbreviations "Tib." and "Skt." respectively.

Dorje Sempa.
Painting by Joseph Duane.

I

The Chikai Bardo

The number of beings wandering in Samsara are as endless as their perceptions, and these perceptions are as limitless as the number of Dharmas. All these Dharmas are contained in the two categories of the Worldly Dharma and the Holy Dharma.

The Worldly Dharma is endless, but as Lord Buddha taught, it is all contained in the *Five Skandhas,* in Tibetan called *pung po nga:* pung po meaning "aggregate;" nga meaning "five."

The Five Skandhas are form, feeling, perception, intention, and consciousness. The six sense organs (eyes, ears, body, nose, tongue, and consciousness) and their objects (form, sound, feeling, smelling, tasting, and sensation) are together the Twelve Born and Increasing Moment, in Tibetan called *Kyi Che Chu Nyi:* Kyi meaning "to be born or arise;" che meaning "to increase or flourish;" chu nyi meaning "twelve." These are the phenomena of samsaric delusion.

The Holy Dharma is endless, but it is all contained in the Hinayana, Mahayana and Vajrayana teachings of the Buddha. In this case, we are referring to the Vajrayana practice, particularly as it pertains to death and rebirth. With this knowledge the Five Skandhas and the five elements transcend into the Five Dhyana Buddhas *(Tathagatas).*

In Tibetan, the word *Bardo* means "intermediate state." There are six different kinds of Bardo. The first is the Bardo of Life, *Kye Ne Bardo;* the second is the Bardo of the Dream State, *Milam Bardo;* the third is the Bardo of Meditation, *Samten Bardo;* the fourth is the Bardo of the Process of Death,

1

Chikai Bardo; the fifth is the State after Death, *Chonyi Bardo*; and the sixth is the Bardo of the Search for Rebirth in Samsara, *Sipai Bardo.*

The Bardo of Life (Kye Ne Bardo) encompasses the experience of the illusion of waking reality. It includes all negative and positive actions during each lifetime from birth until death. The Bardo of the Dream State (Milam Bardo) includes all mental activity while the physical body is sleeping. The Meditation Bardo (Samten Bardo) includes the myriad of meditation experiences from the lowest levels of realization to the attainment of enlightenment. These meditative experiences range from one-pointed concentration to the states of non-meditation.

The Bardo of the Process of Death awaits us all. Even now we should begin preparing ourselves for the enormous difficulties, the pain and anguish we will experience. Most of us do not want to die, and many of us will not even allow ourselves to think about it. Yet it is certain that we all must die. Even the Buddha and those who attained enlightenment after him, all passed away. As they did, so must we all pass away.

The great yogi of Tibet, *Milarepa,* was an enlightened being who could transform himself into the four elements, and yet, he also passed away. In fact, if we examine our own situation, we see that we are far from being free of illusion, ignorance, hatred and all the negative qualities that may be associated with human existence. How then can we say that we will not die?

Even as death is certain, we must also remember that it is not painless. It is not like having the flame of a candle blown out by the wind or extinguished with water. Very few people are able to die with great peace and happiness, even those who have sincerely and conscientiously practiced the Dharma and have, through meditation, achieved great power over their own minds.

So, if death is certain we must also be prepared for the consequences. How can we best face our ultimate fate? Basically, there are two ways. The first is to practice the Dharma with great compassion for the benefit of all sentient beings. The second is to gain control of our mind through intense devotion. With these two we can overcome all obstacles.

Whatever we possess, our relatives, our best friends, all our wealth will be useless to us when we die. During our lives, most of what we do caters to the desires of our bodies. Yet, when death occurs we must leave the body on which we have spent so much effort. At that time only our consciousness experiences the results of past actions. When we are alive our body depends on the five basic elements for existence. We know that we get sick or feel uncomfortable if there is any slight change in the balance of the five elements. For example, if it is too hot, we get sick; if too cold, we get sick. Yet, at death these five elements upon which we depended are left behind.

Our physical existence, which relies on the five inner elements, flesh, bodily fluids, bodily heat, breathing, and bodily complexion, corresponds to the five outer elements, the earth, water, fire, wind and ether. At the time of death, the five inner elements gradually dissolve into one another and in order not to be afraid at this time you should know what stage the dissolving is in. This dissolving is called in Tibetan (Thimrim). Each of these dissolving stages has the enlightened aspect represented by each of the five Female Buddhas. The female Buddha *Sangye Chenma* is the pure transcending element of the nature of the earth and in bodily systems, the flesh. The female Buddha *Mamaki* is the pure transcending element of the nature of water and in bodily systems, the body fluids. The female Buddha *Go Karmo* is the pure transcending element of the nature of fire and in bodily systems, the body heat. The female Buddhas *Damtsik Drolma* and *Yingchogma* are the pure transcending elements of the air and ether, respectively, and in bodily systems, breath and body complexion.

If during your lifetime you have experienced the development and completion stages in meditative concentration on the deities, then in the Bardo, by realizing mind itself is emptiness, you can recognize the dissolving stages and have the opportunity to be released from suffering and attain enlightenment.

The process begins as the element earth dissolves and is absorbed by the element water. This is accompanied by the inner experience that all phenomena take on a yellow appearance. You will envision and experience that everything is falling apart from great floods and earthquakes. You will not be able to stand because your strength is fast disappearing. At that time you should try to identify and meditate that the yellow things you see and your mind are one, without any independent existence. In other words, if you can transcend the duality, then you can attain the level of enlightenment of the female Buddha called Sangye Chenma. If you lose this great opportunity, painful experiences in Samsara will continue.

In the second phase, the element water dissolves and is absorbed by the element fire. This is associated with the inner experience of all phenomena taking on a white appearance. Externally, you will experience the sensation that the entire universe has been flooded with water. During this time, those around you perceive that your face and lips are rapidly drying up. You will also feel extremely thirsty. If, when this takes place, you are able to meditate with complete conviction that whatever you see as water and whiteness is all a product of your mind, with nothing existing independently, then you will attain enlightenment and achieve the state of the female Buddha Mamaki.

When the third element, fire, dissolves into the element air you will have the inner experience that everything is red, and will experience the sensation that everything around you is burning. During this time, the heat from your body will go away. If, at this moment, you can meditate one-pointedly that the external and internal experiences are all mind-created and that nothing exists independently of mind, then you will accomplish enlightenment and attain the state of the female Buddha Go Karmo.

However, if you do not achieve this stage, the element air will dissolve into ether itself. When this happens, you will *Verbal experience during homage July 4, 19* have the inner experience of greenness and then the external experience that all phenomena in the universe are being blown away by the winds of a great storm. You will hear a grinding roar like that of a thousand thunders. At this moment, meditate one-pointedly that all the lights, sounds and colors you are experiencing are created by your mind and that nothing exists independently. If you are able to realize that the mind itself is emptiness without any independent existence, then you will attain enlightenment and achieve the state of the female Buddha Damtsik Drolma.

If you do not achieve this stage, ether will dissolve into consciousness itself. At this time, you enter a very deep darkness and lose sensory perception. Meditate one-pointedly and identify your mind as the nature of *Dharmadhatu*, or clear light. You will then attain enlightenment, the state of the female Buddha Yingchogma.

At this point all the five elements have dissolved and you will not be able to move any part of your body. First the external air or breath will be extinguished. Then you will see a *14, p. 16* small white *bindu*, the *Bodhicitta,** appearing at your forehead and descending slowly; this is the male Bodhicitta, the symbol of skillful means. When the white bindu descends, you will see all phenomena turning white. At that moment, all the thirty-three different kinds of anger will be extinguished in a flash, and even if you have had great anger, for example the anger you may have felt toward someone who killed your father, it will be completely extinguished. At the same time you will experience the Wisdom of Joy, which is the very essence of the *Nirmanakaya*. The impure body upon transcendent purification becomes the Nirmanakaya, in Tibetan

---

* In this context, Bodhicitta (Tib. *Chang Sem*) implies the essence of the pure mind and is not to be confused with the compassion generated for the benefit of all beings, expressed by the same term. It appears as a *bindu* or "point of light."

Trul Ku. This is the divine body of incarnation and the body of the spiritual state in which abide all great teachers and all Bodhisattvas' incarnations on earth. The Nirmanakaya represents the Wisdom of Joy which is beyond dualistic grasping. If you can experience and recognize this joy and wisdom, you will gain enlightenment and attain the state of Dorje Sempa, the essence of the body of all the Buddhas. Then you will not be lost in the Bardo.

After this you will see a red bindu rising slowly from your navel. This is the female Bodhicitta, the symbol of wisdom. When the red bindu rises, you will see all phenomena around you turning red. During that time, all of the forty types of desire will be extinguished and even if you see the most attractive god or goddess, you will have no desire. At that moment you will experience the Wisdom of Supreme Joy, which is the esence of the *Sambhogakaya.* The impure speech upon transcendent purification becomes the Sambhogakaya, in Tibetan *Lon Ku.* It is the divine body of perfect endowment and symbolizes the state of spiritual communion in which all Bodhisattvas exist, transcending the ordinary realm. The Sambhogakaya represents the Supreme Joy, which is a deeper and more profound and permanent joy. If you can realize this extraordinary joy and wisdom, you can attain the state of *Amitabha,* the essence of the speech of all the Buddhas, and you will not be lost in the Bardo.

If you are not successful in meditating and attaining enlightenment in this stage, you will see the red and white bindus approaching one another and eventually meeting at your heart *chakra.* As they meet you will experience an opaque darkness, as on the night of the new moon — very dark — and the seven kinds of ignorance and delusion will cease. At that moment you will have the supreme experience of Wisdom Beyond Joyfulness and immediately you can transform yourself into the mind of all the Buddhas, which is *Vairocana.* The dualistic mind upon transcendent purification becomes the *Dharmakaya,* in Tibetan *Chö Ku.* It is the fundamental truth in which

all dualities merge into transcendent oneness and is beyond
sensual perception. The Dharmakaya is Wisdom Beyond Joyfulness. It is beyond conceptualization, more profound and in-
destructable. At that moment, one does not have to make an
effort to meditate; it comes spontaneously and naturally. If
you are unable to realize the essence of the mind of all the Buddhas (Vairocana), then you fall back into Samsara. However,
if you are able to have this realization, then you will attain
enlightenment and have no need to wander further in the
Bardo.

The essence of the body of all the Buddhas is Dorje Sempa, *Om*
the essence of the speech of all the Buddhas is Amitabha, the *Ah*
essence of the mind of all the Buddhas is Vairocana. Vairocana *Hung*
represents the source of all Buddhas.

If you cannot attain enlightenment at this moment, then
you will be lost in the Chonyi Bardo. Whether you will
wander in the Bardo or catch the spark of enlightenment of the
three states described depends on the practice of the Dharma
and the meditation you do in this lifetime.

All sentient beings have essentially the same experiences
when they die. The differences will depend on their ability to
recognize the true nature of the various stages. This in turn will
depend on their training and practice of meditation. When the
red and white Bodhicitta meet at the heart chakra, a person
who has accomplished very deep and profound meditation in
this lifetime will realize the true nature of mind. There will be a
spontaneous recognition that the mind which has been meditating on emptiness and the state of emptiness itself are one
and the same. Each will mutually recognize the other. The
mind which meditates on emptiness during the lifetime is called
the son; the natural reality of the mind itself is known as the
mother. The person who has accomplished very thorough and
profound meditation will experience a merging of the two.
This is like the encounter between a mother and a long-lost
child. When the mother and child meet each other, the mother
will naturally and spontaneously recognize her child and be

filled with a natural joy. At that moment she will lose all other awareness and experience only the happiness of recognizing and meeting her child. When you realize the emptiness of the mind and also the emptiness of the realization, then you attain the highest enlightenment, Dharmakaya. In Tibet, some great Lamas and Yogis who have experienced the state of Dharmakaya may sit up two or three days in meditation posture after death. When very highly-realized Lamas die, they will often stay in that posture after death, meditating for from three to seven days. When the meditation is over, they have realized enlightenment, and the body will collapse. This is a sign that they have attained realization.

There are two different ways of obtaining enlightenment when you die. These two depend on two different ways of meditating. They are form meditation *(Kye Rim)* and formless meditation *(Dzok Rim)*. If you meditate on form you will gain enlightenment in the following way. You will see the meeting of the two bindu in the form of deities *(yidams)*. For example, the white bindu may be seen as a yidam with male aspects, *Chakrasamvara*. Similarly, you will experience the red bindu as the female deity, *Vajrayogini*. You will have the realization that these two deities, male and female, are your root yidams and by praying to them with faith and devotion you will receive empowerment from them. At that moment you will see vividly the forms of the two yidams and when your consciousness dissolves into the heart center of the yidam and becomes inseparable from it, you will attain enlightenment. You will receive outer, inner and secret empowerments from these two deities. Because of the virtuous power of your devotion and also by the power of compassion of the yidams on whom you meditated, you will attain enlightenment. This, of course, depends on whether or not you have profound devotion and long experience in meditating on the deities.

If you meditate on formlessness, you will experience enlightenment as the meeting of the two Bodhicitta bindus. This is the realization of high Lamas.

Uninitiated lay persons who see the meeting of the two bindus will glimpse the form of their next rebirth in the six realms. If they are to be born as human beings, animals or hungry ghosts, they will have the feeling that the white bindu is their future father and the red bindu is their future mother. If they are to be born in the lower states of existence they will react with great fear. They will become unconscious for about three and a half days, then go to the Chonyi Bardo where they will become aware that they are dead.

According to the pandit *Atisha* and also *Ma Chik Labkyi Drolma,* at the moment you see the form of your next rebirth, you will also see certain wrathful and peaceful deities. If you can recognize these deities at that moment, you will become inseparable from them and attain enlightenment. All this depends on your meditation and on your Dharma practice.

This description of the Chikai Bardo is not contained in the English translations of the *Tibetan Book of the Dead (Bardo Thodol).* The teachings are scattered throughout the many great Tibetan books, but do not exist in an edited form in the manner presented here. Everything that I have been talking about is part of the oral transmission which I received from my teacher. Now that you have received the teachings you are certain about the future. You have the freedom to do positive or negative actions. It is up to you to decide which will be of most benefit. You know that positive actions lead to happiness and negative actions lead to unhappiness. Now I have told you.

*   *   *

During the Chikai Bardo there are three different possibilities for attaining enlightenment according to your superior, mediocre or inferior capabilities. If you have superior ability through meditation practice, you will realize that death and life are both created by the mind. If you are able to recognize that both are illusions, you will understand the nature of your mind, and achieve liberation. Mind itself is emptiness. A person of the superior state will come to the conclusion that happiness, unhappiness, death, birth, good, bad, and all such things partake in this emptiness and are mere creations of the mind. If you are able to recognize this, you can gain enlightenment.

The middle level of beings can achieve liberation by the transfer of consciousness. This method, called *Phowa*, or "consciousness transference," is an extremely profound teaching. It is even possible for a person who does not have deep experience of the Dharma to be liberated immediately by the Phowa that the Lama conducts during the Chikai Bardo. *Tilopa*, a great Yogi of the *Kagyu Order*, said that Phowa is the only method in the Dharma where a being can be liberated without profound meditation experience. He also said that for the proficient meditator, death is not really dying but the path to enlightenment. If you have had Phowa instruction and have practiced it faithfully, it is possible to achieve liberation through this means without the aid of a Lama.

However, before you initiate the process of consciousness transference you must be absolutely certain that you are dying. Otherwise you will kill yourself and suffer the attendant harmful karmic consequences. For those who have had some Tantric initiations and practice meditation, the body becomes a dwelling place for different Tantric deities. Premature practice of Phowa is the same as suicide, and will cut the bond with these deities. Phowa instruction can be given only by a Lama to a student who has fulfilled certain requirements. The student must have completed *Ngöndro* or the Eight *Nyung Nes*. If one has not had the Phowa instruction, his consciousness may be transferred by a Lama at the time of death. It is best if the Lama is with the dying person, but he may still perform the ceremony from a distance. The relatives must be absolutely certain he is dying before they notify the Lama. The exact time for giving the Phowa is right after the external breathing has stopped and just before the internal breathing ceases. It is important to call the Lama in time so that he can prevent the consciousness from escaping the body as there is no benefit in giving the Phowa after this.

There are nine different openings through which the consciousness can escape. The route through which the consciousness escapes determines the future rebirth. If it escapes through the anus, rebirth will be in the hell realm; if through the genital organ, the animal realm; if through the mouth, the hungry ghost realm; if through the nose, the human and *yakya* (spirit) realms; if through the navel, the realm of the desire gods; if through the ears, the *asura* or jealous god realm; if through the eyes (including the third eye), the form god realm; and if through the top of the head (four finger-widths back from the hairline), the formless god realm. If the consciousness escapes through the crown of the head (the Opening of Brahma) the being will be reborn in *Dewachen*, the western paradise of Amitabha. With the exception of this last opening, all the other pathways should be blocked.

Karmic accumulation also determines the length of time the consciousness remains in the body. If you have done many unskillful deeds, your consciousness will escape the moment that you stop breathing. Once it has left the body, it is very difficult to call back. In Tibet, in previous times, there have been some Lamas like Milarepa and *Drugpa Kunleg* who could call the consciousness back into the body, but today it may be very difficult to find such Lamas.

Once the Lama has been informed about the death of a person he will immediately meditate upon *Chenrezig* and himself as one, while visualizing in his heart a lotus, a moon and the letter HRI. From the HRI in the Lama's heart, eight smaller HRIs are sent forth to the dying person to block the openings through which the consciousness might escape. Only a Lama with great concentration can do this from far away. If he is on his way to the dead person, he will meditate constantly on Chenrezig and send HRIs in order to prevent the escape of the consciousness. If the consciousness is not kept within the body, it will be lost in Samsara in the cycle of existence. When

the Lama arrives at the place where the person has died, he
visualizes that the dead body is the body of his yidam or deity.
He then goes into deep meditation and begins to give instruc-
tions to the dead person about the Bardo of the Process of
Death. Following this, the Lama, by means of Phowa, will try
to awaken and elevate the consciousness toward liberation. At
that time the person's consciousness is many times more acute
and intelligent than during his lifetime. Because of this
heightened state, whatever is told to the dead person will make
a very deep impression. They will also know thoughts in the
minds of people around them, and understand whatever language is spoken. For example, if an American is dead and a
Tibetan Lama gives instruction, does Phowa, or reads the *Bardo Thodol* in Tibetan, the American will be able to understand
all of these. In this moment the dead person has a natural intel-
ligence that enables him to understand many things at a level
beyond the intellect. If the Phowa is successful, certain signs
will appear on the top of the head. The signs are a drop of
blood or perhaps a small bump. Until these external signs appear, the Lama will keep giving Phowa. If the dead person has
done many unskillful deeds and has broken his commitment
with the Lama, these signs may not come at all. In that case the
Lama will read repeatedly the *Bardo Thodol.*

Questions

**I have read that these Bardo teachings have been closely
guarded secrets for over a thousand years. Why are you now
giving them so freely?**

During Venerable Kalu Rinpoche's last visit to America, the
members of his San Francisco center, Kagyu Droden Kunchab,
sincerely requested Rinpoche to bestow the initiation of the

Hundred Deities of the Bardo. Following the initiation, many disciples asked for the Bardo teaching. Rinpoche said to me, "Now it is time." For this reason I gave the Lung and am now presenting this instruction.

Are we not going through the first three Bardo states every moment of our lives?

Yes, we experience the Bardo every instant and it is because we don't recognize it as such that we are here, in this existence. The Bardo ends when enlightenment begins.

In the part where the red and white bindus mix together is there one state of mind that is male and another female?

These are conventional symbols normally used to describe a particular stage of your realization of emptiness. Thus, they do not represent state of mind, but causative forces. If one achieves realization while meditating on white Bodhicitta, the essence of all the Buddhas' bodily attainments, the deity of Dorje Sempa is attained. If realization is achieved while meditating on the red Bodhicitta, the essence of all the Buddhas' speech attainments, the deity of Amitabha is attained. The white bindu also symbolizes the skillful method of compassion and the red bindu, wisdom. At the instant the two merge in your heart, the lifetime meditative experiences of emptiness and the all-embracing natural reality become one. If this is realized, a state of Mahamudra is achieved.

Um

ah

Hung

How long should the body of the person who has had some initiations be left without touching it?

The ideal time is seven days, but if that is not possible, three and one-half days is enough.

If there is no Lama available to conduct the Phowa, which is often the case in the West, what meditation can the dying person do himself, to help the consciousness exit through the highest path?

There are quite a few things that one can do to be ready to face death. While still alive, one should do very seriously the Ngöndro, or eight successive Nyung Nes. After that, one should get the Phowa instruction from a qualified Lama. If he is successful in Phowa, a sign will be observed on the top of his head. The appearance of the sign depends upon one's faith in the Lama, the strength of one's devotion and the degree of seriousness with which one has practiced purification.

What happens to a person who undergoes a rapid violent death, such as an accident or the like?

In sudden death all experiences are the same; they just occur more rapidly. The moment of death is uncertain. This is precisely why the Buddha and the Lamas preach the law of impermanence. They also say that one must practice the Dharma right now, because death is uncertain. Much depends on what one is thinking at the moment of the accident. If one's general inclination and practice is toward negative thoughts or actions, then, of course, one is likely to experience suffering and confusion. If on the other hand, one is trying to practice compassion, meditation on stilling the mind and positive actions recommended by the teachers, then of course, one will not fail.

What is the difference between internal and external breathing?

External breathing is breathing from the lungs through the nostrils to the outer air. Internal breathing is internal vital processes, centered in the heart, which continue after outer breathing stops.

Is it possible for a person to commit suicide while thinking positive thoughts?

Definitely not. It is impossible for beings to kill themselves while in a positive state of mind. This is a contradiction in terms. If through practicing meditation, a person has reached some level of understanding, he will reflect on the suffering of all beings and wish to continue working for their liberation. He will not delude himself into thinking that good will result from the evil act of killing. There are some places where ritual suicide is held in high regard. In such places, pride in one's image after death is often confused with some kind of realization. But Buddhas never kill themselves.

What happens to the consciousness of a person who dies

while they are asleep, or in the astral body?

There are many subtle forces which come under the category of consciousness. Even during sleep or a trance state, while some components of consciousness may be separated from the physical body, other forces remain. If the body is disturbed, these forces cause awareness to return instantly, to participate in the fate of the physical body. For this reason, it is not possible to die without knowing that death is taking place.

What is the best way we can help someone who is approaching death if they have no experience with the Dharma?

As the person approaches death you should sit quietly with him, generate compassion for all sentient beings, and pray with devotion to all enlightened beings. Make your mind still and try to meditate on spontaneous transcending awareness. If you are unable to achieve the state of emptiness, recite quietly for his benefit the *Sutra of the Thirty-five Buddhas*, which will help him to purify negative karma. Then recite the mantras of the Five Dhyana Buddhas as well as those of all the other deities you know, especially "Om Mani Peme Hung." After this, it is important to repeat the *Bardo Thodol* as many times as possible. During the reading you must generate Bodhicitta and devotion to enlightened beings. If this is done in the proper spirit, it may be possible for him to reach enlightenment merely by hearing the teachings for the first time. But, you must have neither doubt nor hesitation or you may negate all the good you are doing.

Would you comment on the Western medical practice of maintaining a person's breathing and bodily functions by artificial means? What consequences does this have on a person's consciousness? In many cases a person who has stopped breathing and whose pulse has stopped and who does not show any vital signs can be resuscitated over many hours and can be technically brought back to life.

You must realize that it all depends on an accurate appraisal of the sick person's condition. Of course, it is good to help save the life of someone who can be saved. But, you must exercise great care in prolonging the life of someone who is certain to die within a day. Such a person is already undergoing tremendous suffering which may be increased by modern medical practices.

Does this mean that pain-killing drugs should not be used as one approaches death?

When the body is in a drugged condition, the mind, veiled with stupidity, cannot concentrate and is easily drawn into the animal realm.

What is the length of time between the stopping of the external respiration and the internal respiration?

It depends upon several different factors. Of importance are such matters as the physical condition before death, the presence or absence of disease, and of course the actual cause of death, such as an accident. It could be as short a time as a few minutes, to several hours or rarely, a full day.

Are there some saints who can sit down and be in one place and radiate light for a number of days or for a long period of time without decaying?

Yes, it is possible. There have been some Lamas who have stayed in the meditation posture for seven days or even longer after death. On some occasions rainbows surround the body during this time. Ordinary people who die and are kept for that period of time would have a bad odor, but instead, the bodies of accomplished beings give off a pleasant fragrance.

Are the visions in the Bardo the same for a person with another religion or no religion at all?

While wandering in the Bardo, everyone has almost the same experiences. But, the degree of recognition depends on one's practice during their lifetime. When one has no religious training, the lights, deities and all the visions pass before him as mere forms and colors that may frighten and confuse him. Habitual tendencies blow his consciousness through the Bardo like feathers in the wind. Without experience and devotion there is no possibility for wise choices.

Is the "Bodhisattva Vow" broken if the physical body disap-

pears at death?

In Tibet there were certain Lamas who were highly accomplished in meditation. Like Milarepa, they spent their lives in solitary meditation and were able to transcend ego attachments. In many cases, at the time of death they dissolved their physical bodies into the rainbow bodies and did not leave any part of the body behind except the hair and the nails. This is a sign of enlightenment and in becoming enlightened you benefit all sentient beings and do not break the Bodhisattva Vow.

After death, does the consciousness ever try to hang onto the body and feel possessive of it?

One's karmic accumulation determines the length of time the consciousness remains near the physical body. When the consciousness tries to re-enter the corpse it is a sign of negative habitual tendencies deriving from attachments to the physical body. The elements have dissolved and re-entry is impossible, but the consciousness may stay near the body or its possessions for weeks or even years.

There is a process by which people who have incurable diseases are frozen in the hope that a cure may be found for them at some future date. What happens to the consciousness when this process is employed?

If the body is frozen before the consciousness has departed, those who have done this are guilty of killing the sick man by freezing him to death. If the body is frozen after death, it is just one more method of disposing of a corpse. The consciousness can never re-enter the body even though it may remain nearby. Treatment of a corpse in this manner may also enhance the attachment of the consciousness to it and increase the suffering of the being by hindering the search for another body.

In the Evans-Wentz translation of the *Bardo Thodol*, there is a passage which says something about, between the cessation of the external circulation and the internal circulation whoever is present at the dying person's side should press the jugular veins on each side of the neck so as to direct the consciousness through the proper exit of the body. Is this ap-

propriate physical action to take to help the dying person?

One who has experience should locate the two jugular veins, or channels in the neck, and press them both at the same time so that the consciousness, being pushed by the wisdom mind, will go straight up through the secret path and be liberated or be born in the upper realms. This is very dangerous for if one does not have experience doing this he may speed up the process of death and kill the person.

Is it possible for a disincarnate being to enter another's body? If this is possible, how can it be kept out?

There are a few kinds of very powerful spirits which are able to enter one's body and disturb one's mind and health. But most spirits do not have this power.

If most spirits try to enter another's body, they will not be able. However, the fact that they have such an intention will have a bad effect on the person whose body they are trying to enter. It could result in suffering and illness. There are two ways to prevent this from happening. If one has received initiation and instruction concerning a wrathful deity and can practice with true compassion, one should visualize oneself as the wrathful deity, and this will frighten the being away with compassionate energy. Otherwise, one should meditate one-pointedly on emptiness.

What is a healthy attitude toward spirits and psychic phenomena?

If you are confronted with spirits, meditate on emptiness if you are able. The spirits will realize that there is nothing for them to harm and leave you alone. If you are unable to do this, and have the appropriate initiation and instruction, meditate on a wrathful deity and recite the appropriate mantra with compassion and devotion.

How does one determine one's yidam?

You must work hard in your practice now in order to accumulate the merit and experience that will enable you to choose your yidam when that stage of your practice arrives.

Mandala of the Peaceful Deities, from Booker Monastery in Tibet.
Photograph by Denis Eysseric-Francois and Rose-Marie Mengual
(Tempa Dargye and Tempa Zangmo)

II

The Chonyi Bardo

We have talked about the first two of the three levels of potential for liberation. A person of the first level gains enlightenment through his own meditation. The person of the second level gains liberation by the practice of Phowa, either by himself or by the Lama. Someone of the third level is not able to succeed in any of these and depends on hearing the *Bardo Thodol*. After he has been dead for about three and a half days, in an unconscious state, he will regain his consciousness and wonder what happened to him. He will feel very strange in a way he has never experienced before. He will see all his relations and friends weeping and will hear them asking him why he has departed. He will try to tell them that he is alive and present, but they will not be able to hear him, because he has only a mental body, although he will believe that it is physical. When he sees people who are enjoying the possessions that he has accumulated with great attachment over his lifetime, he will be angry and very jealous.

In Tibet it is a common practice to call Lamas to perform certain rites and *Pujas*. If any of the Lamas are not mindful while performing these mantras and visualizations, the dead person will know this and will lose his faith in the Lama and the Dharma. It is very important for the Lamas to concentrate deeply at this time.

When the dead person walks out into the sun, he has no shadow; when he looks into a mirror he sees no reflection. In this way he learns that he is dead and becomes sorrowful and afraid. At this moment he realizes that now he cannot take with him whatever he has accumulated over his lifetime. He must leave everything behind including his friends, his family members and even his own body.

Because of the human tendency to place great value on the body, the consciousness hovers around the dead body trying to re-enter. However, the body that he sees is the form of the animal symbolizing the calendar year in which he was born. For example, if he was born in the year of the tiger he will see the dead body of a tiger. The consciousness will feel very possessive of that body and although it tries to enter, it cannot.

The body is dead in the sense that the five elements which constituted the functioning organism are no longer present. After three and one-half days the dead body is taken away to be buried, cremated, or otherwise disposed of. Then the consciousness realizes that it needs another body and it begins to search for one. Once the body has been left behind the consciousness can travel anywhere and can penetrate anything (except the *stupa* in Bodhgaya, because it became impenetrable by the power of the Buddha's prayer).

The consciousness possesses great power in the Bardo: if you are able to think about the pure land of Great Bliss (Dewachen), then you can gain instant liberation. But, because of the force of Karma most of us will not be able to focus on such high thoughts and will instead be possessed by fear, sorrow and negative feelings. This is the time when previous unskillful deeds harm you and skillful deeds can help. Now you must depend on all that you have done in your past lifetimes. Even if you realize that the fruits of negative actions are poisonous, you are unable to throw them away. At this moment, your name, good health, fame, beauty, wealth, and whatever you have accumulated in previous lifetimes will be of no value to you. You are completely dependent upon previous actions. Sometime after, everything becomes blue like the sky. In the middle of the sky you will see a throne being carried by eight lions. On this throne you will see Vairocana who is white, in divine embrace (yab-yum) with the female deity Yingchokma. As you see all this, a very bright blue light will emanate from the heart of Vairocana who is the pure form of the aggregate of consciousness. A white light of lesser brightness will also shine before you from the god realm. This dim white light is the light of the deliberate ignorance that you have accumulated in your previous lifetimes. The blue light which emanates from the heart center of Vairocana is the light of the space of Dharma Wisdom (Dharmadhatu). When you see these two different lights you will be very frightened by the light coming from Vairocana. Because of habitual tendencies of deliberate ignorance, you will be very attracted to the dim white light from the god realm. It is a manifestation of your past karma. If you follow the white light, then you will be re-born as a god. Although this may sound positive, in reality you will be lost in the cycle of existence and will experience nearly endless suffering. You must not follow the dim white light to which you are naturally attracted, but try to follow the blue light. You should feel gratitude for the fact that Vairocana with his great compassion has come to liberate and help you. If you think positively in this way, trying to seek help from Vairocana, then your own mind and the light emanation of Vairocana will merge and become one. In this merging you attain the level of enlightenment of a Sambhogakaya Buddha.

Between the first and second day, because of the power of deliberate ignorance and conflicting emotions, you may become frightened and try to escape from Vairocana's light. If you do not achieve liberation, the next cycle of deities, those of Dorje Sempa (Skt. Vajrasattva), blue in color, makes its appearance. White light from the pure form of the water element, the essence of Mirror-like Wisdom, emanates from Dorje Sempa's heart. Simultaneously, because of your habitual

Vairocana sits in the Enlightened Mudra,
showing the enlightened Buddha awakening.

tendencies of anger, dim, smoky light will shine forth from the hell realm. Dorje Sempa appears from the eastern realm of Perfect Joyfulness *(Ngönpargawa)*. He is holding a *dorje* and bell and is seated on an elephant throne embracing his consort, Sangye Chenma. He is accompanied by two Bodhisattvas, *Jampa (Maitreya)* and *Sai Ningpo*. There are also two female Bodhisattvas with him, *Lhasema* and *Pupuma*. Thus there are six deities appearing at this point.

From the heart of Dorje Sempa and his consort, who are the pure aspect of the skandha of form, Mirror-like Wisdom, white light flows into the heart of the dead person. Due to past negative karma you will desire to escape this wisdom light and follow the light from the hell realm. You must remember that it is the light of wisdom and compassion with which you must merge, all the while generating intense devotion for Dorje Sempa and praying for his guidance through the terrors of the Bardo. Although the dim smoky light, through the power of anger accumulated since beginningless time, will exert an enormous attraction for you, it will only lure you into the unbearable suffering of the hell realm. If you have complete faith in Dorje Sempa, his compassionate wisdom will merge with the natural reality of your own mind, and in this way you will attain the enlightenment of a Sambhogakaya Buddha of the eastern Buddha realm of Perfect Joyfulness *(Ngönpargawa)*.

If you are not liberated, the power of anger will draw forth the next cycle. The Buddha, *Rinchen Jungne* (Skt. *Ratnasambhava*) appears in the southern realm. The light emanating from him is yellow and represents the pure form of the element earth. He holds a precious jewel and sits on a horse throne with his consort Mamaki. In his retinue are the two Bodhisattvas *Nam Kyi Nyingpo*, essence of space, and *Kuntuzangpo*, the All-good One. There are two female Bodhisattvas, *Malema*, goddess of ornaments, and *Dhupema*, goddess of incense. These will all appear in the midst of rainbow light. The yellow light pouring forth from their hearts is a manifestation

Dorje Sempa sits in the Earth-Touching Mudra,
showing the overcoming of obstruction.

of the skandha of feeling in its pure form, the Wisdom of Equanimity.

The dominant yellow light is very bright, luminous and clear, punctuated by many discs of light of various sizes. This streams out of the hearts of Ratnasambhava and his consort and penetrates your heart. At the same time dim, blue light shines forth from the human realm.

Because of the power of pride we are afraid of the yellow light and attracted to the dim blue light, the essence of pride and the source of passion and mental disturbance. If you become attracted to the blue light, you will fall back into the human realm to endure the sufferings with which we are all so familiar.

Instead you should strive to conquer your fears and perceive the yellow light as the manifestation of the Wisdom of Equanimity. With one-pointed devotion to Ratnasambhava, merge your mind with the light and let it rest in a natural state. Try to realize that the light of wisdom coming from the Buddha and your own mind are of the exact same nature; there is no difference between them. If you attain liberation on this third day, you will become a Sambhogakaya Buddha in the southern realm (Paldangdenpa). If you do not, your wanderings in the Bardo continue as you enter the fourth phase.

On the fourth day Amitabha and his retinue appear. The bright red light emanating from the heart of Amitabha and his consort is the pure form of the element fire as well as a manifestation of Discriminating Wisdom. It is also the light of the skandha which is associated with perception. Amitabha appears in the western Buddha realm of Dewachen (Skt. Sukhavati), with a lotus flower in his two hands. His body is red and he sits on a peacock throne holding his consort Go Karmo. In his retinue are two male Bodhisattvas, Chenrezig and Jampeyang, and the two female Bodhisattvas, Girtima and Alokema. All six appear in the midst of a shining rainbow.

At the same time that the brilliant red light shines from Amitabha into your heart center, the dim yellow light of desire

Ratnasambhava sits in the Supreme Giving Mudra,
showing the elimination of fear and obstacles on the path.

and greed streams forth from the realm of hungry ghosts. Because of accumulated negative karma, you may be afraid of the red light and take pleasure in the softer yellow light. You must strive to overcome your attraction to this and focus your mind one-pointedly on the brilliant red light of Amitabha. If you are able to identify the light of wisdom and merge your consciousness with it, you will attain the enlightenment of a Sambhogakaya Buddha of the western realm (Dewachen).

Even if you are not able to achieve liberation, pray to Amitabha with intense devotion. Through his boundless compassion, Amitabha has the power to assist beings in achieving the wisdom state and to draw them toward his glorious light.

If because of your habitual tendencies of desire, you were unable to achieve liberation, you wander into the fifth day when the Buddha *Amoghasiddhi* appears with his retinue in the northern realm. The bright green light emanating from Amoghasiddhi is the pure form of the element air and a manifestation of All-accomplishing Wisdom. It also is the light of the skandha of intention.

The Buddha Amoghasiddhi is green and appears holding a double dorje. He sits with his consort, Damtsik Drolma, on a throne supported by *shang-shang* birds, who have human forms with wings and feathers. He is accompanied by two male Bodhisattvas, *Chana Dorje* and *Dripanamsal,* and the two female Bodhisattvas *Gendema* and *Nirtima.* They all appear surrounded by blazing light amidst a multitude of rainbows. At the same time that the green wisdom light streams into your heart, the dim red light of intense jealousy pours forth from the realm of the jealous gods. You must avoid this dim red light with all your strength and focus your mind on the light of Amoghasiddhi. If you are able to meditate upon him one-pointedly, with great devotion, your mind will merge with his rainbow image and you will become a Sambhogakaya Buddha in the northern realm *(La Rab Zog Pa).*

If you have not yet achieved realization, you will enter the sixth day, when, as a result of the combination of the five poi-

Amitabha sits in the Meditation Mudra,
showing equanimity.

sons, all five Buddhas will make their appearance together. Again, you have the opportunity to attain liberation by recognizing the light as the light of wisdom and merging your mind with it. Along with the wisdom light, shine the lights of the six realms of existence.

During this phase of the Bardo, the elements earth, fire, water and ether (excluding air) make their appearance, accompanied by their respective lights, each blazing with great intensity.

The Buddhas and their consorts are arrayed in the form of a mandala. The Buddha Vairocana, white in color, appears in the center; Vajrasattva, blue, appears in the east; Ratnasambhava, yellow, appears in the south; Amitabha, red, appears in the west; and Amoghasiddhi, green, appears in the north. In addition to these, male and female protectors appear in each direction and in the center. Other Buddhas come from each of the six realms.

The protectors in the four directions are known as the "four doorkeepers of the mandala" and each have their own name. The male protectors are named as follows: The first, in the eastern direction, is called *Nampargyelwa*. In the southern direction the gatekeeper is called *Shingishig* or *Yamantaka*. In the west, the doorkeeper is *Hayagriwa*. In the north the gatekeeper is called *Dutsikyilwa*. There are also four female gatekeepers: In the east is *Chakkyuma*, in the south is *Shakpama*, in the west is *Chakdroma*, and in the north is *Drilbuma*. Totally surrounding this mandala of the four gates there are six Buddhas. The first Buddha is the Buddha of the god realm and he is called *Gyajin*. The second Buddha is the Buddha of the jealous gods and he is called *Tagzang*. The third one is the Buddha of the human realm and he is called *Shakya Senga*. The fourth one is the Buddha of the animal realm and he is called *Senge Rabten*. The fifth one is the Buddha of the preta (hungry ghost) realm and he is called *Kaparma*. The sixth one is the Buddha of the hell realm and he is called *Chogyi Gyelpo*. The primordial Buddha, called Kuntuzangpo, with

Amoghasiddhi sits in the Giving Refuge Mudra,
showing supreme protection.

his consort, *Kuntuzangmo*, also appears.

All together, there will be forty-two deities in the mandala; all are manifestations of your own mind shining before you. You must strive to understand that these Buddhas only appear to come forth from the Buddha realms; in actuality the entire mandala emerges from the four directions within your own heart, with the center of the mandala as the fifth direction (also inseparable from your heart). The Buddhas shine due to the power of your own mind. However, even though they are the manifestation of your own mind, it is still necessary for you to first come to this realization. You should also know that they are all the essence of your yidam, your personal deity with whom you have merged during your practice throughout your life.

Again, from four of the Buddhas, the sharp, shining yet subtle wisdom light which surrounds them streams forth toward your heart center. The four wisdoms which shine are: the Wisdom of Dharmadhatu; the Mirror-like Wisdom; the Wisdom of Equanimity, and the Wisdom of Discrimination. You should realize that these lights have appeared as the manifestation of your own mind and try to merge your mind with them. It is very important to have neither great attachment nor great aversion in the mind at this point. If you are able to quell all discursive thought and merge your mind with these four wisdoms, then the true essence of voidness will shine on you and you will attain liberation. At this point it is not possible for the fifth wisdom, All-accomplishing Wisdom, to shine forth because you have not yet understood the true nature of voidness.

During this period it is very crucial to remember any teachings you have heard throughout your lifetime. This is of extreme importance. Earlier you will recall we employed the metaphor of a son and mother. Similarly, the meditation practice that you have carried on during your life and the instruction that you have received on the generating stage (the generation of the deities) and the concluding stage (natural reality) is analogous to a son; the natural state itself is analogous to a mother. If you have been meditating and if you can remember your meditation practice at this point, it will be like a mother meeting her long-lost son. At this point of recognition, all of your previous practice bears fruit, and in integrating the practice with the Bardo experience, you can instantly attain enlightenment. If you can achieve this state, you will reach the *samadhi* which is called *"gyun gyi ting ngi dzin"* which is a continuous unbroken state of meditation.

At this time, the light of wisdom from the four Buddhas and also the light of passion coming from the six different realms are both shining together. The lights from the six different realms are white (deliberate ignorance), red (jealousy), yellow (greed), blue (pride), green (ignorance), and smoky black (hatred). Although you will feel great attachment for these lights, you should reject them without adverse feeling, all the while maintaining a sense of equanimity. You must pray one-pointedly to the five Buddhas because even one moment of attachment to those lights from Samsara will cause you to be reborn in one of the six realms. If this occurs, there is very little chance to gain a human form and to achieve liberation.

At this point there are three possible ways of attaining liberation. One is to recognize the wisdom light and to merge with it; the second is for the light to draw you into itself; and the third way is through the combined power of intense devotion on your part and the great compassion of the Buddhas. Liberation is possible because we are able to hold our mind in a state of one-pointed devotion; the compassion of the Buddhas is also a manifestation of mind, therefore, these two can merge in enlightenment. The importance of devotion, practice and prayer during your lifetime cannot be over-emphasized.

The five Buddhas will shine for all beings because all beings are composed of the five skandhas. Seeing the Buddhas is simply another way of perceiving the skandhas. Light shines from the five female consorts because they are the manifestation of the five physical elements which make up the body.

Since the bodies of all beings depend on these five elements, the five female consorts will definitely appear. Their light will shine for all beings, but not all beings will be able to recognize them. If you can recognize them, then there is the possibility of gaining liberation; however, if you cannot, which is usually the case, you will continue to wander in Samsara.

*   *   *

On the seventh day, the Knowledge-Holding Deities (Rigdzin Lhasok) appear, sending forth light of different colors. The colors symbolize the pure aspects of the five wisdoms which are the antidote of the five poisons. Through the power of negative karma, you may be afraid. However, this is a great opportunity to recognize the wisdom lights and escape from Samsara by merging with them.

Subsequently, a pure land, Dakpacachod, appears in a blaze of rainbow light, in the midst of which you will see the red Knowledge-holding Deity, Pema Karkyi Wangchuk, and his consort. They are standing in dancing posture, in divine embrace. At the same time you will see another deity in the east whose name is Sala Nepai Rigdzin. He and his dakini are white in color. In the south is Tsela Wang Wai Rigdzin and his dakini who are yellow. In the west appears Chag Gya Chenpo Rigdzin and his dakini who are red. In the north appears Lunki Drubpai Rigdzin and his dakini who are green. All of these five deities and their dakinis appear in their wrathful aspects. All have wrathful ornaments and are in dancing posture. Surrounding all five deities are numerous dakinis; further away are dharmapalas. The sky is filled with deities who have come to help those whose vows have been kept on a perfect level. They have also come to punish those who have not kept their vows or maintained good relationships with their teachers. As before, whatever reactions you might have toward the manifestations of the deities and the different lights are all a product of your consciousness.

Powerful lights emanate from the five deities and pierce your heart. Simultaneously, a dim green light shines forth from the animal realm. Due to your habitual tendencies of ignorance you will be more attracted to the green light. You will be frightened by the wisdom light and try to escape. At this point you must concentrate and meditate on the wisdom light and pray that you will be saved. If, because of your devotion, prayer and meditation in the past you are able to merge with the wisdom light, you will be born into the pure land of Dakpacachod. Those who have done form meditation according to the Vajrayana tradition should be able to reach this pure land within seven days after death. In this phase of the Bardo, all of the deities and the lights will emanate from your throat center.

If you are not successful in achieving enlightenment by this time you will move to the next stage where you will experience the more wrathful aspects of the Bardo. On the eighth day you will see the Buddha *Heruka*. He is dark brown and has three faces, six hands and four feet. The right face is white, the left is red and the central face is brownish purple. Lights stream from his body. In front of him is a dakini called Buddha *Tro Di Sho Rima*. They are in divine embrace. You will hear a grinding roar like thunder. From his body blaze the fires of wisdom. He is sitting on a throne supported by a *Garuda*. This particular deity, who is the wrathful aspect of Vairocana, will emanate from the center of your brain. If you recognize him, meditate that he is your yidam, and your mind and the deity will become inseparable. As a result of this realization, you will achieve the enlightenment of a Sambhogakaya Buddha.

If you are not able to accomplish this you will see another deity on the ninth day. He is called *Vajra Heruka* and he has three faces, six hands and four feet. His consort, called *Vajra Tro Di*, is before him in dancing posture. This deity and his dakini are the wrathful aspect of Dorje Sempa. If you recognize that this is Dorje Sempa and do not become frightened of the wrathful appearance, you will gain enlightenment.

If you do not, the tenth day will come and you will experience *Ratna Heruka* and his dakini. He is dark yellowish black and has three faces, six hands and four feet. He has nine eyes. He is embraced by his consort *Ratna Tro Di*. They are the wrathful aspect of Ratnasambhava. If you recognize them as such and merge with them, you will gain enlightenment.

On the eleventh day, you will see *Pema Heruka*. He also has three faces, six hands and four feet. In front of him in dancing posture is his dakini called *Pema Tro Di*. These together are the wrathful aspect of Amitabha Buddha and if you recognize them as such and take refuge in them, the image of this heruka and his dakini and your mind will become one and you will gain enlightenment.

On the twelfth day, you will experience *Karma Heruka* who also has three faces, six hands and four feet. In front of him is his dakini, *Karma Tro Di*, in dancing posture. This deity is the wrathful manifestation of Amoghasiddhi. If you recognize him as such and take refuge in him you will obtain enlightenment on the twelfth day.

As there are a number of deities who appear after these five herukas with their consorts, we will now make some generalizations about them. There are eight deities called *Gaurima*. There are eight *Takenma*. There are four dakinis serving as doorkeepers. There are twenty-eight *Wang Chuk Ma*. This constitutes a total of fifty-eight Wrathful Deities.

There are forty-two Peaceful Deities. The Rigdzin Lhasok are not counted in the One Hundred Bardo deities. This refers to the knowledge-holding deities that appear on the seventh day who are neither peaceful nor wrathful.

The sound that you will hear from these fifty-eight wrathful deities, "HUNG! PHAT!", is like that of a thousand thunders. If you have had some experience in meditation upon such wrathful deities you will recognize the sound and the deities and you will not be afraid. In this way you will realize the nature of these deities and will therefore gain enlightenment. If you do not have the experience of meditation upon the wrathful deities, you should at least have read the *Bardo Thodol* concerning the true nature of these deities; because of this you may be able to recognize them and react accordingly. If you are able to recognize these deities as your yidam, take refuge in them with devotion, and generate compassion for sentient beings, you will be able to gain enlightenment in the pure land of Perfect Joyfulness.

Depending upon your connection with the deities during your lifetime, you have the opportunity of attaining enlightenment during your remaining days in the Bardo. If you do not achieve liberation in the Chonyi Bardo, you will wander on into the Sipai Bardo.

So as we have seen, all the Samsaras are produced from the five skandhas, each skandha having its own characteristics.

The first skandha of form is characterized by destructibility and breakability. The essential characteristic of the skandha of feeling is desire or the act of experiencing. Moment-to-moment cognition and the mind's following after objects is the essential characteristic of the skandha of perception. The essential characteristic of the skandha of intention is performing actions and gathering propensities. Perception and the creation of objects are the essential characteristics of the skandha of consciousness.

These are the five worldly skandhas of desire which explode in all the conflicting emotions and thus create the various kinds of actions. The results of these actions will be limitless suffering in Samsara. These five skandhas are on an impure level. When you purify your perceptions, the five skandhas transform into the five Dhyana Buddhas, each of the skandhas represented by each of the Buddhas.

When purely perceived, the skandha of form becomes the Buddha Vajrasattva *(Akshobya)*. Likewise, the purified perception of the skandha of feeling becomes the Buddha Ratnasambhava. The pure skanda of perception is the Buddha Amitabha. The skandhas of intention and consciousness purely perceived become the Buddhas Amoghasiddhi and

Vairocana, respectively.

The Buddha Vajrasattva does not have color or shape so is separate from the skandha of form. Buddha Ratnasambhava is not attached to experience so is separated from the skandha of feeling. Buddha Amitabha is without intention or aim and does not distinguish or discriminate and so is separate from the skandha of perception. The Buddha Amoghasiddhi is without motivation and so is separate from the skandha of intention. There is no holding or grasping to objects or phenomena so the Buddha Vairocana is separate from the skandha of consciousness.

Each of the five Dhyana Buddhas has a consort which is one of the five female Buddhas. Their Sanskrit names are given here in parenthesis. The consort of Vairocana is Yingchokma *(Akasadhatis)*; the consort of Akshobya is Sangye Chenma *(Logana)*; the consort of Ratnasambhava is Mamaki (Mamaki); and the consorts of Amitabha and Amoghasiddhi are respectively Go Karmo *(Pandaravasini)* and Damtsik Drolma *(Tara)*.

Questions

Could you explain again why the Vajrayana is the secret path?

According to the Vajrayana, it is possible to gain instantaneous enlightenment. If you have practiced diligently during this lifetime you will recognize instantly the shining lights of the Buddhas and attain enlightenment in one moment. If you have not achieved high states of meditation, but have a great deal of devotion and compassion you still may be able to gain enlightenment in the Bardo.

The teachings are secret because very few people can comprehend them. To avoid producing wrong views among those who might misunderstand, the teachings are presented only at the appropriate times to those seeking knowledge of this path. Only those who are eligible through training and practice may receive certain initiations. It is possible for those with merit and devotion to attain enlightenment through the experience of an initiation.

If a lama gives initiations and teachings to the spiritually immature, his ability to benefit all sentient beings may be hindered. A student who takes teachings and initiations and who subsequently breaks his commitment will completely block his path to enlightenment by these wrong views. If he influences other beings to follow his own wrong views, he commits actions of grave karmic consequence and destroys his precious opportunity to follow the enlightened path.

How does the breaking of commitments to the Vajra Master block the path to enlightenment?

All knowledge and all experience reside in the Vajra Master and it is only through him and his teachings that we are brought to an understanding of the enlightened path. If through wrong views we destroy our bond with him, we repay the medicine of his kindness with poison. In the Tantric scriptures it is said: *"Without the lama, the name of Buddha is not heard."* For a thousand *kalpas* (fortunate eons), a thousand Buddhas have achieved enlightenment through the Lama.

Do the deities relate to certain centers in our bodies?

The peaceful deities come forth from the heart center; the wrathful deities come from the brain; the knowledge-holding deities come from the throat. All are manifestations of mind and should be seen as such.

Could you please repeat the Five Wisdoms?

The Five Wisdoms are: the Wisdom of the Dharmadhatu (the essence of reality or essence of the universe), Mirror-like Wisdom, the Wisdom of Equanimity, the Wisdom of Discrimination and the All-accomplishing Wisdom. These Five Wisdoms are not something external, but come from within ourselves and are the purified aspects of the five poisons. Ignorance is the cause of these poisons: desire, anger, jealousy, pride and greed.

Before coming to the teaching this evening I spent some time with a friend who is pregnant and has decided that if she doesn't have a miscarriage this week, she will have an abortion. I was wondering if you could say anything about any special way of being of assistance to both the baby and the mother.

The best thing for you to do would be to try to talk her out of the abortion because it is an act of profound negative consequences to kill a human being. A human being's body is so precious that it would be better if you could talk her into having the baby and then putting it up for adoption. There are many organizations who will help a woman do this. If you do so, this will be an act of considerable merit and will increase your good fortune.

If she has the abortion anyway, what can be done to help the child?

If you know beforehand when it will take place, tell a Lama so he can pray for the baby. Perhaps the people in the Dharma Center can do some practice and dedicate the merit for the baby.

Lama, you were saying that you should try to be attracted to blue light and to avoid the white light. So should we try to merge our consciousness with the blue light or with the mind of Vairocana?

If you have had meditation experience, and react with devotion and gratitude, you will be able to meditate that the light and the image of the Buddha are inseparable with your mind. In this way you will reach the non-dualistic state and achieve the enlightenment of a Sambhogakaya Buddha.

I would like to know the difference between Amitabha Buddha and Amitayus?

Both are basically the same nature, but they have different functions. The activity of Amitabha Buddha is such that if we pray to him with devotion and recite his mantra, then by the power of this prayer we will be born in Dewachen, the western paradise of great blessings. The activity of Amitayus is such that prayers to him grant a long life and good health.

How do the elements and the skandhas relate to the deities?

The elements represent female Buddhas. The skandhas represent male Buddhas.

Lama, you spoke about consciousness leaving the body through different routes which would determine rebirth. Would you see Vairocana if your consciousness left through a route other than the secret route, or does that whole process happen before the visualization of the different deities?

The deities appear in the manner described, but your perception of them is conditioned by your karmic background, which influences the route through which your consciousness passes.

You speak of many realms of enlightenment. Does that mean that there are different levels of enlightenment?

One becomes enlightened in a Sambhogakaya realm due to the influence of one's accumulated merit and wisdom. Enlightenment in any Sambhogakaya realm is complete and perfect enlightenment. The realms exist as skillful means of liberating beings of different karmic accumulation.

If the Dharmakaya is the sun, then the Sambhoghkaya is like the sun's rays. We cannot say they are separate. Without the sun there are no rays. The Nirmanakaya has the same relation to the Sambhogakaya. All three kayas are the Dharmakaya. Therefore, enlightenment in any realm is merging the mind with the Dharmakaya.

It is said that Chenrezig emanates in his wrathful Mahakala form particularly to help beings in the Bardo. If one does the practice of Mahakala with faith, devotion, and concentration in this lifetime, where in the Bardo will he manifest to protect us?

To one who has sincerely done the practice of *Mahakala*, all the wrathful deities of the Bardo will appear in Mahakala's form, and because of habitual tendencies, the practitioner will easily recognize them. The practitioner will feel joy at the sight of Mahakala, and will feel confident in his protection, and be without fear. Then he can easily merge his mind with Mahakala, and achieve liberation.

Mandala of the Wrathful Deities, from Booker Monastery in Tibet.
Photograph by Denis Eysseric-Francois and Rose-Marie Mengual
(Tempa Dargye and Tempa Zangmo)

III

The Sipai Bardo

During your wanderings in the Sipai Bardo you will have certain miraculous capacities deriving from past karma. These will include such powers as being able to pass through anything, including mountains and the walls of buildings. Nothing will be able to stop you because you are in mental form.

At this time you will have four experiences unlike anything you had during your life. First, you will be caught in the midst of a great rainstorm. Second, you will experience a tremendous wind of unbelievable force. Third, you will experience intense total darkness. Fourth, you will hear noise so loud that you may become frightened.

What is experienced in the Bardo signifies the past life habits. The rainstorm signifies the past life habit of desire. The wind signifies the past life habit of anger. Darkness is ignorance, or not knowing the truth, from beginningless time. The noise is the combination of all the habits of conflicting emotions which in the Bardo makes you frightened and disturbs your concentration. This hinders a favorable rebirth which would enable you to achieve enlightenment.

This is followed by a series of nine experiences, divided into three groups. Depending on your karmic accumulations you will have perceptions associated with one of these groups. If you have done many positive deeds you will perceive yourself inside of a lovely palace suited for a god. Or, you may find yourself in a very tall building, or sitting on a very high throne. If you have accumulated neither very much positive or negative karma, you will experience the inside of a thatch-roofed house, or a house with a roof of leaves, or find yourself in the midst of a bound sheaf of rice stalks. If you have acquired very little merit you will be inside tall green grass or experience trying to crawl through small holes broken in the walls of crude huts, or in a dense jungle.

Because of individual karma and the significance of the truth of karma and the results of negative and positive actions, there are four different ways to be reborn in the six realms: from a womb (human being); from an egg (certain animals); as a result of the attraction to heat (certain insects); and from instantaneous transformation (certain gods). This last example is a result of great merit, but yet not perfect merit since conflicting emotions still remain. There are some similarities between classes of birth, particularly birth from wombs and eggs. Beings who are born out of heat do not undergo the sufferings of a baby in his mother's womb. *Devas*, as a result of meritorious actions, miraculously appear from lotus flowers. Instantaneous transformation can also occur in the case of beings born in the hell realms immediately after death.

In the Sipai Bardo, wisdom lights do not appear. Instead, lights of different colors shine forth from the six different realms of existence. As the time for rebirth approaches, the dead person experiences a pleasurable attraction for a particular light. If he is going to be reborn as a *deva* (god), he will be attracted to the white light and he would have the feeling that he is entering a great heavenly palace. If he is going to be born as a jealous god he will be attracted to the red light and have the feeling that he is passing into a lovely garden or a place of superb natural beauty. If he is going to be reborn as an animal, he will be attracted to the green light and experience passing into a cave. If he is going to be born as a hungry ghost, he will be attracted to the yellow light and feel he is entering a heap of burned wood. If he is going to be reborn in the hell realm, he will take pleasure in the smoky light. He will see a black and red house and he will hear a very beautiful melody which he can barely resist. Even at this point there are ways by which you can avoid entering into these various forms of rebirth.

When lights and other phenomena appear, meditate one-pointedly that they are a manifestation of Chenrezig, the embodiment of the compassion of all the Buddhas. In this way your devotion will merge with Chenrezig's compassion and you will reach enlightenment.

If you are unable to achieve liberation because of karmic veils, strive to follow the blue light of the human realm. Human birth can occur in four different continents or separate planes of existence. From the Buddhist point of view, the world exists as the mountain Meru in the center, surrounded by four continents. Each continent has different realms and different kinds of beings caused by individual karmas. If you are to be born in the eastern continent you will see beautiful men and women around a lake. You should not wish this birth because, although you would have a rich, long and happy life, there will be no Dharma and no chance for enlightenment. If the western continent is to be your birth place, you will see fine mares and stallions around a lake. Again, you must not desire birth in this continent because it also offers a rich life with no possibility for practicing the Dharma. If your birth will occur in the northern continent, you will see beautiful trees and gardens around a lake. Here again, you would have a rich, happy and long life with no opportunity to practice Dharma. If you have not succeeded in attaining liberation in the three levels of the Bardo and find yourself searching for a human birth, strive to find a womb in the southern continent where you will see many beautiful houses. This is the only continent where the Dharma can be found and practiced. If you are to be born there you will recognize your future parents in the act of intercourse, no matter how far away they may be.

If you are to be born a male, you will be attracted to your mother and have aversion for your father. If you are to be born a female, you will be attracted to your father and have aversion toward your mother. At the moment you have these feelings, you will enter the womb and be born as an ordinary being.

There are two ways in which rebirth as a human being can be prevented. You can attain liberation by realizing that the houses and the blue light are merely projections of your own mind which are illusory in nature, *Mahamaya*. In the second way, you reach the non-dualistic state by realizing that both the light and the mind which perceives it are devoid of any inherent reality; they are emptiness.

Consciousness as it wanders in the Bardo is frequently symbolized by a red-hot iron bar. The flexibility of the bar in this state is analogous to the condition of the mind separated from the physical body. Once the iron cools, the previously imposed form solidifies. In the same way, by the force of the karmic wind of habitual tendencies, you create the thoughts which determine future patterns of mental activity. In the Bardo the power of a single positive thought can guarantee your enlightenment; conversely, a single negative thought can draw your mind into the depths of suffering from which escape is of the utmost difficulty.

Tulkus in the Sipai Bardo

There are two basic classes of *tulkus*, ordinary and superior. An ordinary tulku, through the power of his virtue and morality during past lives, may be reborn with a precious human body. However, he is still subject to the winds of karma and therefore cannot choose freely the means whereby he will benefit beings. If he continues to practice Dharma he will develop Bodhicitta; but even at this point, it is still possible for habitual tendencies to assert negative influences and result in his falling into the lower realms. Many of these beings remember something of their past lives.

A superior tulku is totally free from the limitations imposed by these residual negative tendencies. He has the power to exert free choice over how he will best benefit sentient beings. He may help beings during the forty-nine days in the Bardo and then choose his future incarnation. He may enter any pure land, or he may choose his rebirth after three or four days of voidness meditation. There are also many other possibilities.

When a tulku, or reincarnated being, reaches this level of the Sipai Bardo, he merges with his yidam, focusing his mind on a HRI in the heart of the deity, who is embracing his consort. Different lights radiate out to all of the Buddhas and Bodhisattvas, and to the peaceful and wrathful deities. They, in turn, send forth light which is the essence of all the Buddhas. This is absorbed through the top of the head, transformed into a white bindu (white Bodhicitta sphere) and passes via the middle vein, which runs vertically through the center of the body, through the secret organ (called the "vajra" in Tantric practice) into the consort's secret opening (called a "lotus"). At this moment he separates from the deity and consort, and if his enlightened energy is to be manifested on a physical plane, a white OM, the essence of his consciousness, comes forth from the consort's secret opening. Light of different colors radiates from this OM to the Buddhas and Bodhisattvas of the ten directions; they descend and are absorbed into the white OM. At this point, through his clairvoyant powers, he will know the characteristics of the wisdom dakini who will be his future mother, and he will enter her womb. He will be born with a beautiful appearance. The very sight of him will inspire joy and peace. Seeing him or even hearing his name can liberate those who have sufficient devotion.

If the enlightened energy is to be manifested on the plane of speech, the same process occurs, except that the consciousness of the tulku will appear in the form of a red AH. He will have a beautiful and melodious voice and be very knowledgeable and extremely adept in explaining the sutras and tantras. The sole purpose of his incarnation at this level is to spread the Dharma for the benefit of all sentient beings.

If the tulku's energy is to benefit beings through the power of mind, everything remains the same, with the exception that a blue HUNG will appear. In this incarnation, he will bring peace and joy to all beings through the activity of his mind. Although he possesses great compassion, he may behave in a wrathful manner when it is necessary. He will be greatly accomplished in meditation.

A yellow SO will emanate if the enlightened energy is to be manifested as the qualities of all the Buddhas. The tulku will benefit many beings through his skill in the five sciences. These are technology, medical science, debating and logic, the science of sound (music and languages), and the inner sciences which refine the mind by utilizing the methods of the three Yanas, Hinayana, Mahayana and Vajrayana. He will have a long, comfortable and happy life and be able to attract large numbers of followers.

In the case of an activity reincarnation, the visualization remains the same except a green HA is emanated. He will be highly developed in form meditation, and have powerful tantra and mantra practices by which he can benefit sentient beings. His mantras will be extremely powerful; he will be able to help sick people and will be able to subdue and exorcise demons or evil spirits.

A tenth-level Bodhisattva can have five incarnations, each with their respective characteristic. All these emanate from the Dharmakaya. A Bodhisattva of the lower levels has other ways to reincarnate, using different visualizations and methods. In the Sipai Bardo, he will visualize the deity without consort. This deity will melt into light and dissolve into emptiness. From the emptiness he will reappear as the letter HRI, or HUNG, or another letter depending on his yidam. This letter will shoot like an arrow into the pure land and he will gain enlightenment.

In order to emanate in these five types of incarnations a lower level Bodhisattva must first attain enlightenment in a pure land.

A great Bodhisattva, even though he has the power to pass into nirvana will, through his compassion, choose to reincarnate. Depending on how he can best serve the needs of beings, he will choose a royal lineage, a *Mahasiddhi* lineage or a birth among ordinary beings, often in a low but meritorious family. Certain noble lineages have produced many generations of great Lamas who have done immeasurable good for all beings. In Tibet these families are held in extremely high regard. Previous reincarnations have appointed dharmapalas who prevent ordinary beings from taking birth in these families.

As a result of their great compassion, some Bodhisattvas are born into poor and even sinful families, to help reduce the sufferings of these beings and aid them in reaching enlightenment; or they may enter a family of ghosts or spirits in order to subdue such beings. Some incarnate as *dakas* or dakinis in their own Bodhisattva family, or in families which have attained liberation by controlling the vital forces within the breath and veins (the completing stage of Tantra). He will encounter the Dharma immediately after being born into such a family and have no difficulty learning and practicing.

A being who has not reached the highest levels of tantric practice sees his future parents as his yidam with consort, from whom he will receive secret initiations. At the moment he perceives this, he generates Bodhicitta, sees the Lama as the yidam and vows to take the secret initiation for the benefit of all beings. He then visualizes the womb of his mother as a *mandala* and meditates that the two bindu emanating from his mother and father are the sun and the moon, respectively. Depending on how he wishes to benefit beings, he will generate the letter to be transferred into the corresponding deity with whose energy he wishes to merge. For example, if he wishes to bestow benefit by compassion, his consciousness becomes a white **HRI** standing on a sun-moon seat. Light radiates from the **HRI** to the Buddhas and Bodhisattvas of the ten directions, who descend to bestow their body, speech and mind empowerments. The **HRI** is transformed into the yidam with whom the being wishes to merge. If he wishes to help others by increasing the Buddha's doctrine, he will meditate on *Shakyamuni*; if he has the desire to benefit others with his knowledge, he meditates on *Manjushri*; if he has a wish to benefit others with compassion, he will meditate on Chenrezig; if power is needed to subdue beings he will meditate on *Vajrapani*; if he wishes to benefit others with clairvoyance and miracles, he will meditate on *Guru Rinpoche*.

When his rebirth takes place, such a being will not experience the sufferings of an ordinary child. When in the womb, he sits in meditation posture, totally absorbed, with no awareness of the pain of growth or the size of his body. His mother experiences great ease and happiness, has good dreams, and sees wonderful omens and signs. She may dream that a dorje has pierced her heart, or perhaps she dreams of a counterclockwise conch shell or a golden wheel. In many cases, she and others hear the sounds of *Om Mani Peme Hung* or other mantras.

The baby will often be born in meditation posture; other times he will say mantras or greet his parents. If this does not occur, it is only because certain impurities in the body of the mother have clouded his purity. In some cases Bodhisattvas will be able to recall past experiences or understand Dharma teachings instantly on the first hearing. During practice, many Bodhisattvas accomplish realization without effort.

Questions

When realization of the illusory nature of phenomena is attained, what happens to the phenomena?

The energy of ego fuels the fires of the five poisons which veil the mind and prevent our seeing reality in its true nature. When enlightenment is attained, all phenomena cease to exist independently of mind: they dissolve into the non-dualistic state, the space of Dharmakaya. However, although fully-realized beings are beyond dualism and non-dualism, they have the power to exist in a dualistic state or a non-dualistic state, depending on what conditions are needed to benefit all sentient beings.

At the moment of being aware of the next rebirth, is there any way that it can be changed or is it an unalterable fact?

It can be changed, but only by the force of all the actions that you do now. If you have accumulated considerable positive karma, then the force of those actions will change it very favorably in your direction. But, if you have done a lot of negative deeds in your life, then of course, it will change for the worse.

Are the choices available to us in the Bardo also determined by how much merit we have accumulated?

There are many forms of past karma that influence the choices we make in the Bardo. The winds of karma are always blowing and the choices we make are naturally influenced by the totality of our past actions. This is why in order to make wise decisions in the Bardo, we must practice now. Then we will see that even the choices themselves are illusory.

When I strive to do good and avoid evil, is not the striving still a result of past karma? Why should I even try?

Your karmic accumulation provides the situation, but every second you exercise freedom to make decisions. With increasing spiritual development, there is more freedom and also increasing awareness of the need to make wise decisions. Once you begin to tread the spiritual path, in some ways your perception of possibilities diminishes. By the time a being approaches the lowest Bodhisattva levels, his choices become very clear. In addition, with spiritual development there are greater and greater abilities to counteract the forces of habitual tendency. We must not drift into the fatalism that prompts us to do what we wish and blame it on our so-called "karma."

Throughout these teachings you have used the word "he" when referring to the highest tulkus. Are there also female tulkus of the highest levels?

Of course.

Is there any difference in the visualization a tulku uses to achieve a female birth?

None whatsoever. Consciousness has no gender. A tulku merely uses whatever vessel will most benefit beings.

Is there any kind of memory associated with the Bardo states? Perhaps one could remember previous experiences in the Bardo states and these memories could influence one's choices.

Since all sentient beings have gone through the Bardo many times, it is possible to have a memory of your past lives, but it would only be a brief flash. You may also have glimpses into your future lives. Through one-pointed concentration, one experienced in meditation will block these thoughts, but for the inexperienced person many illusions will appear, producing fear and confusion. You may remember in flashes the past Bardo, but these memories provide no help in making choices.

Sometimes I read about Lamas who choose their own moment of death because they feel that their body is no longer useful. Could you tell us something about that?

It is possible to do this if the Lama has already attained enlightenment. Everything he does is for the benefit of sentient beings so he will only use his power to determine the fate of his body if there is a good reason to do so. But a Lama like this is very rare. His Holiness Dalai Lama, His Holiness Karmapa, His Holiness Sakya Trizin, His Holiness Dudjom Rinpoche and His Holiness Kalu Rinpoche and certain others have such power. These Lamas have the freedom to live or die depending on how they can most benefit beings.

If a Lama decides to be reborn as a human being, does he go to Ratnasambhava to be reborn, or is there another way?

Bodhisattvas do not have to wait until the appearance of Ratnasambhava. This is only the means for ordinary beings to achieve a human birth. The karmic accumulations which result in a human birth also dictate one's perceptions in the Bardo. Consequently, one sees the light of Ratnasambhava and is drawn toward the human realm at the same time.

For what length of time does one who has reached the Mahamudra state remain in the Bardo?

There are basically four types of Mahamudra practitioners: 1) one-pointed, 2) state of absolute non-activity, 3) state of unified taste (co-existence of both relative and absolute), and 4) state of non-meditation. There are three further subdivisions within each of these categories, but now we will speak only generally.

After death, beings who have reached the first three levels may leave their bodies seated in meditation posture for three or more days, during which time they are in a state of clear light. The consciousness of such beings enters the Bardo, but only for a short time after which they become enlightened. Beings who have achieved the highest level of Mahamudra have completely transcended meditation and for them there is total freedom immediately after death. For instance, Milarepa, who attained the state of non-meditation, understood that the nature of mind is voidness. For him there was no more need to meditate, to learn, or to do practice: He was enlightened.

Does the realization enable you to attain enlightenment, or do you get enlightened by your karma?

Training for the realization has to begin now. For example, if you meet a person you have never met before, then you will have no chance of recognizing him. Your recognition of the deities in the Bardo depends on your spiritual training and practice now; this in turn enhances the virtuous power that enables you to realize enlightenment. Similarly, if at the moment of death you remember the Lamas who explained the teachings to you and have faith in them, then through the power of devotion, you will be able to recognize enlightenment. Other Vajrayana initiations can also give you the power to attain realization. So you must have faith and devotion as well as a relationship with the Vajra Master (Lama), according to the vows *(damtsik)* that you take during the initiations and teachings you receive from the Lamas.

What is the highest means of accumulating merit to achieve enlightenment?

The best method is to practice the *Six Paramitas* (generosity, morality, patience, diligence, meditative concentration, and wisdom) with a Bodhisattva attitude. In other words, whatever good you do is for the benefit of other sentient beings. That will lead to Buddhahood. Those who accumulate merit for the purpose of being born in the next life as a better human being or one with wealth and power, or as a god, are attached to Samsara. This is not the right path to enlightenment.

How does our practice help other beings?

You should meditate with the intention that you are doing it for the benefit of all beings, not just for yourself. The energy of that beneficial thought will go out to beings. The more pure the thought, the greater is the energy associated with it and the greater the purifying effect. Therefore, you should have in your mind at such moments that you are practicing for the sake of all that lives. If anyone says "I" am going to achieve enlightenment, this grasping prevents him from reaching a non-dualistic state. Complete enlightenment is for the sake of other beings.

May these teachings bring many benefits to those who have interest in the Dharma. May the merit of giving these teachings be dedicated to the long life and flourishing activity of those who hold the Buddha's doctrine in this world. My thanks to all who have read these teachings.

Appendix

Kuntuzangpo with His consort Kuntuzangmo.
Line drawing by Roberta Bell Ehrlich.

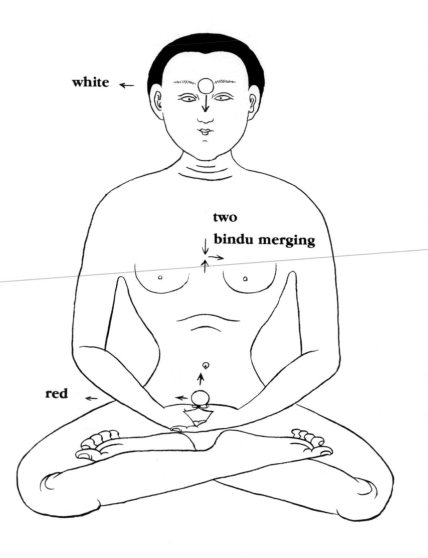

Chikai Bardo: the bindus (points of light) and their paths. Enlightenment is attainable by superior meditators.

Line drawing by Wangyal of Dolpo.

Element	Dissolves into	Essence	Experience Inner	Experience Outer	Possible to attain state of female Buddha:
EARTH	Water	Flesh	Yellow	Falling apart	Sangye Chenma
WATER	Fire	Bodily fluids	White	Floods	Mamaki
FIRE	Air	Bodily heat	Red	Burning	Go Karmo
AIR	Ether	Breath	Green	Windstorm	Damtsik Drolma (Tara)
ETHER	Consciousness	Bodily complexion	Blue	Grinding roar	Yingchokma

Chikai Bardo: the five elements dissolve. Enlightenment is attainable by superior meditators.

Location:	Forehead	Navel	Heart
Color:	White	Red	Blue
Bodhicitta embodies:	Male	Female	
Symbolizing:	Skillful Means	Wisdom	
Can experience:	Wisdom of Joy	Wisdom of Supreme Joy	Wisdom Beyond Joyfulness
Essence of:	Nirmanakaya	Sambhogakaya	Dharmakaya
Attain state of:	Dorje Sempa (Vajrasattva)	Amitabha	Vairocana
Essence of Buddhas:	Body	Speech	Mind
Extinguishes:	33 Angers (descending)	40 Desires (ascending)	7 Ignorances

Chikai Bardo: the bindus and their paths.

Body Opening	Realm of Rebirth	
Anus	Hell	
Genitals	Animal	
Mouth	Hungry ghost	
Navel	Desire gods	All openings except crown of head should be blocked to reach enlightenment by Phowa.
Ears	Jealous gods	
Nose	Human and yakya	
Eyes	Form god	
Top of head	Formless god	
Crown of head	Dewachen (western paradise of Amitabha)	

Chikai Bardo: the openings of the body through which the consciousness can leave, and the corresponding realms of rebirth. Enlightenment attainable by medium-level meditator.

Family	Buddha	Vajra	Ratna	Padma	Karma
Direction	Center	East	South	West	North
Male Buddha	Vairocana	Dorje Sempa (Vajrasattva)	Ratna-sambhava	Amitabha	Amoghasiddhi
Female Buddha	Yingchokma	Sangye Chenma	Mamaki	Go Karmo	Damtsik Drolma (Tara)
Skandha	Consciousness	Form	Feeling	Perception	Intention
Element	Ether	Water	Earth	Fire	Air
Wisdom	Dharmadhatu	Mirror-like	Equanimity	Discrimination	All-accomplishing Wisdom
Bright Light	White Body Blue Light	Blue Body White Light	Yellow	Red	Green
Dim Light	White	Smoky Black	Blue	Yellow	Red
Poison	Deliberate Ignorance	Anger	Pride	Greed Desire	Jealousy
Realm	God	Hell	Human	Hungry Ghosts	Demi-gods

Chonyi Bardo: the five Buddha families and their associations.

Family	Five Wrathful Buddhas
Direction	Mandala: all directions
Male Buddha	All Knowledge-holding deities
Female Buddha	Wrathful consorts of all wrathful Tathagatas
Skandha	All combined
Element	All combined
Wisdom	All combined
Bright Light	Multi-color
Dull Light	Green
Poison	Ignorance
Realm	Animal

Chonyi Bardo: the Wrathful Deities.

Color	Syllable	Symbol	Level
White	OM		Body
Red	AH		Speech
Blue	HUNG		Mind
Yellow	SO		Quality
Green	HA		Activity

Tulkus in the Sipai Bardo: symbols which appear when a tulku is choosing the focus for his next life.

Visualization:	Benefiting Others through:
Shakyamuni	Increasing doctrine
Manjushri	Knowledge
Chenrezig	Compassion
Vajrapani	Subduing evil
Guru Rinpoche	Clairvoyance

Tulkus in the Sipai Bardo: correspondence of visualization in the womb with the tulku's intention.

Glossary

BINDU Bindu are aspects of the yogic body (inner energies, physical and non-physical) that are meditated upon in advanced Vajrayana practices.

BODHICITTA Relative bodhicitta arises from the practitioner's meditation upon and generation of compassion for other sentient beings (see *Bodhisattva*). This leads to glimpses of ultimate bodhicitta, the ultimate true nature of reality. In turn, this inspires more compassion for beings and the intent to deliver them from Samsara.

BODHISATTVA Bodhisattva literally means "pure enlightened attitude." In general this term is applied to anyone who has taken the vow to relinquish their personal enlightenment in order to work for the benefit of all other sentient beings. More specifically, it designates a special class of beings who have not only taken the above vow but who also have attained a significant degree of realization on the path, from the first level *bhumi* to the tenth level Bodhisattva. The basic idea is the generation of an attitude of putting the welfare of other beings above one's own welfare.

BUDDHA Buddha means the state of being which is completely clear and unstained by the defilements of attachment, aversion, and ignorance. Also, it refers to the attainment of all-pervasive wisdom. This word may denote the historical Buddha, Shakyamuni, or the principle of enlightenment within sentient beings.

CHAKRA Chakra is a complex systematic description of physical and psychological energy channels.

DAKINI Dakini refers to certain female meditational deities or non-physical beings. Dakinis can also be celestial messengers or protectors.

DEITY Deities are a manifestation of enlightened wisdom. They arise from the Buddha's infinite compassion and wisdom. They may take peaceful or wrathful forms in accordance with the individual personality and the great variety of mental states represented by sentient beings. Their purpose is to subdue mental and emotional defilements on the path to enlightenment.

DHARMADHATU Dharmadhatu is the all-encompassing space in which all phenomena of any sort arise and fall, without beginning or end.

DHARMAPALA This class of deities' main purpose is to preserve the teachings of the Buddha and protect the practitioners of Dharma from obstacles encountered on the path to enlightenment.

DORJE This symbolizes the indestructible and inexhaustible mind, refined and free from the conflicting emotions.

GARUDA This mythical bird symbolizes the fearlessness of the profound teachings of the Buddha and especially the Vajrayana teachings.

LUNG Lung is ceremonial reading of a sacred text by the teacher which transmits the blessings of the lineage and authorizes the student to study that text.

MAHAMUDRA Literally "maha" means "great," "mu" means "wisdom emptiness," and "dra" means "all." It is often translated as "great symbol." Therefore, one may say it is the Great Wisdom-Emptiness under which all phenomena, samsara, and nirvana exist. It is a special transmission which embodies the most complete enlightenment.

MANDALA The word mandala may refer to a symbolic representation or map of a meditation visualization (palace of deities) or to an offering to the deities or one's guru. This offering is imagined to be limitless and as splendid as Mount Meru and the four continents containing the five desirable things of the human and god realms.

NGÖNDRO Ngöndro literally means "preliminary" and is used to describe the four extraordinary practices traditionally done at the beginning of a student's Dharma practices. They consist of 100,000 prostrations, Dorje Sempa Mantras, mandala offerings, and prayers to one's guru or lama; the purpose is to purify the body, speech and mind of the individual in order to realize the Mahamudra stage.

NYUNG NES This two-day meditation retreat is done every month during the full moon. The Thousand-armed Chenrezig is the principle meditational deity. The eight precept vows are taken for each twenty-four hour period and the Thousand-armed Chenrezig Sadhana is performed three times each day. It is said that practicing eight of these retreats bars the individual from rebirth in the lower realms forever.

SAMADHI Samadhi describes a one-pointed involvement in meditation. There are many kinds of samadhi, but the term does not infer anything about realization or enlightenment. Also, it does not indicate what the object of meditation is.

SAMSARA Samsara includes the six realms of existence. These are characterized by the suffering which results from attachment, revulsion, and ignorance. Samsara is often symbolized by depicting the six realms on a wheel, indicating the cyclical nature of existence.

SKANDHAS Skandhas are sometimes referred to as the five "psycho-constituents of reality." They are form, feeling, perception, intention, and consciousness, and together they comprise an individual's total life experience. When they are purely perceived or transcended, each one is related to one of the five Buddha families.

STUPA This structure is built as a memorial to the principle of enlightenment and often contains relics of past enlightened beings.

TANTRA This complex term encompasses vast possibilities. Generally, it refers to the meditational systems of the Vajrayana which can lead to enlightenment in one lifetime for those who are able to devote themselves to the practice.

TRIKAYA The Dharmakaya, Sambhogakaya, and Nirmanakaya are the three spheres (Trikaya) or planes of buddhahood. The Nirmanakaya is the worldly sphere where enlightenment takes the form of a human being, e.g., one's own guru or the historical Buddha Shakyamuni. The Sambhogakaya is a special sphere not of this physical world, but accessible to humans through various practices, including meditation on deities, mandalas, and one's own guru. The Dharmakaya is the sphere of enlightenment itself, beyond concept, without physical characteristics or reference of any kind, e.g., the guru's mind.

TULKU This refers to an incarnate lama or to the embodiment of the principle of enlightenment.

TWELVE BORN AND INCREASING MOMENT The "twelve born" are the six sense organs (subject) and their objects. The subject attracts the objects and at that moment, emotions (e.g. — anger, desire, etc.) arise and increase.

YIDAM Literally, "yi" means "mind" and "dham" means "tight." This refers to a strong mental connection with deities (see *deity*); more particularly, this word is associated with personal meditational deities.

Bibliography

(1) *The Tibetan Book of the Dead.* Francesca Fremantle and Chögyam Trungpa Rinpoche. Shambala, Berkeley and London. 1975.

(2) *The Tibetan Book of the Dead.* Lama Kazi Dawa-Samdup, translator. W. Y. Evans-Wentz, editor, Oxford University Press, New York. 1971. (Third edition: 1960.)

(3) *The Opening of the Wisdom Eye.* His Holiness the XIVth Dalai Lama. The Theosophical Publishing House, Wheaton, Illinois (reprint 1974).

The Heartfelt Prayer of Devotion to Vajradhara, Rung Jung Kun Kyab (Kalu Rinpoche)

The innate wisdom obscured by clouds of the five poisons,
By non-awareness violating the conduct of Dharma,
Through error, dwelling solely in conditioned activity,
Lord of Love, look upon beings of this troubled age with compassion.

Just in meeting you, the conflicting emotions are pacified;
By the medicine of your nectar-like speech, hope and fear are dispelled;
Just bringing you to mind, deluded appearance is exhausted;
Buddha taking human form, look with eyes of compassion.

Your own nature is the perfect Dharma Body of the Buddha,
Yet from compassion for beings you have manifested the Form Body,
For the benefit of beings, vast as space, your load is great,
Bodhisattva, Son of the Victorious One, look with eyes of compassion.

Beings difficult to teach in countries of many languages,
You lead on the path to liberation by your many skillful means,
Giving the rain of Dharma according to the individual capacities of
    disciples,
Guardian of Shakyamuni's teaching, look with eyes of compassion.

I pray that from this time until enlightenment
Not being separated from the compassionate circle of the Vajra,
You remain continuously ornamenting the crown of my head,
In the present, bardo, and all future existences, I take Refuge in you.

During a time of physical sickness in the year 1982 this poem was composed by the Kagyu Lama known as Karma Lodö Chö Pel, Lodö Gyatso or Lodö Rinchen. During this time of illness when I was confined to a sickbed and finding it uncomfortable to go about or lie down, unbreakable devotion to the body, speech, mind, blessing and activity of the Lama arose and this poem was sung. I pray that whatever arises is seen as the blessing of the Lama.

Translation by Dan Jorgensen (Karma Sherab Tarshin).

Biographical Note

Lama Lodö was born in Sikkim in 1939. At the age of eight he entered a monastery to study the traditional subjects of the Karma Kagyu tradition: reading, writing, religious texts, singing and dancing. At fifteen he met Drupon Tenzin Rinpoche, who was the great meditation master of the The-Yak Monastery and a teacher of His Holiness the sixteenth Gyalwa Karmapa. With his teacher's blessing, Lama Lodö eventually began the traditional three-year retreat, which is a requirement of becoming a lama. Unfortunately, both student and teacher became ill during this time; Tenzin Rinpoche directly contributed to Lama Lodö's recovery, but died himself.

The Lineage-holder of the Karma Kagyu tradition, H. H. Karmapa, intervened during this painful period in Lama Lodö's life. Since he was without a teacher and his study seriously interrupted, His Holiness directed Lama Lodö to seek a new teacher in the Very Venerable Kalu Rinpoche, whom he called the Great Master of this age. Very soon Lama Lodö was able to pass his examination and begin a new retreat. He contracted tuberculosis, but was able to complete his retreat and recovery by viewing the illness as the purification of bad karma.

Lama Lodö has spent the years since then giving instruction in meditation, Dharma and puja. In 1974, H. H. Karmapa and Kalu Rinpoche sent Lama Lodö to the West; he has taught in Belgium, Germany, Holland, Norway, Denmark and Sweden, and since 1976 has been in residence as Senior Spiritual Teacher at the Kagyu Droden Kunchab Center in San Francisco. He teaches extensively on the West Coast.

May it be victorious! I am not so knowledgeable, but I have met the greatly learned and accomplished Lama, and thereby know a little about virtue and non-virtue, and here I have explained it for the benefit of all. By this virtue, may the doctrine-holders live long and may their activity increase. May the sufferings of our parents in the six realms be pacified; may they meet with happiness and finally achieve Buddhahood.

In the Vajrayana vows, it is said that to show the secret path to an inappropriate vessel is to break the vow. But since I have received permission from Venerable Dorje Chang Kalu Rinpoche, I have not broken the vow.